*How to Travel Like a Girl*

# *How to Travel Like a Girl*

**Nita Love**

Copyright © 2025 Nita Love
All Rights Reserved.
No portion of this book may be reproduced in any form without written permission from the publisher or author, except as permitted by U.S. copyright law.

ISBN: 979-8-3493-2160-3

Disclaimer: Solo travel can be unpredictable and involves inherent risks. The author and publisher of this book are not responsible for any injuries, losses, or damages that may occur during or as a result of solo travel. The information and advice provided in this guide are intended to be general guidance only and may not be applicable to every individual or situation. Travelers should always research before embarking on a solo journey. Additionally, travelers should exercise caution and consider their own physical and mental well-being, as well as any health or safety concerns, before engaging in solo travel. By reading this book, you acknowledge that you understand and accept these risks and release the author and publisher from any liability.

This book is Dedicated to:
My Beautiful daughter, Adina
- lovingly nicknamed Chicken -
who has been my faithful companion on countless adventures, never once hesitating to join me on a new journey. This book is dedicated to you, with love and gratitude for the memories we've shared and the many more yet to come.

# *Contents*

Dedication **iv**

INTRODUCTION **1**

1 ME, MYSELF & I **2**

2 GIRLS TRIP, OR NAH? **6**

3 WRITING YOUR ITINERARY **9**

4 WHERE TO GO **12**

5 FUNDING YOUR TRIP **19**

6 LODGING **31**

7 TRANSPORTATION **36**

8 CRUISING BABES **45**

9 EXPAND YOUR HORIZONS **49**

10 RECOGNIZE TOURIST TRAPS **52**

11  UTILIZE DAYLIGHT HOURS  **56**

12  LISTEN TO YOUR GUT!  **60**

13  SHARE YOUR LOCATION  **70**

14  PROTECT YOUR BELONGINGS  **73**

15  PET ACCOMODATIONS  **79**

IN CLOSING  **84**

16  BONUS SECTION- PACKING ESSENTIALS  **87**

17  BONUS SECTION- WHERE TO EAT  **89**

18  BONUS SECTION- STRANGERS  **91**

19  BONUS SECTION- PERSONAL SAFETY  **94**

20  BONUS SECTION- ITINERARY  **96**

21  BONUS SECTION- PLACES TO GO  **99**

About the Author  **110**

# INTRODUCTION

The wait is over! It's time to turn your travel dreams into reality. With the right strategies and tools, you can start planning your dream vacation or take smaller, starter trips that will eventually lead to the ultimate getaway. This book is your comprehensive guide to making travel accessible, safe, and unforgettable. Whether you're a solo adventurer or a group traveler, this guide is designed for you - empowering you with expert tips and secrets to make your travel aspirations a reality.

Travel Like a Girl is more than a guide—it's a pact between women who refuse to let fear dictate their access to adventurous freedom!

"Adventure awaits beyond the horizon, but safety is our compass." – Unknown

# { 1 }

# ME, MYSELF & I

Have you ever dreamed of embarking on a solo adventure, but hesitated due to fear, doubt, or societal expectations? You're not alone. For too long, women have been discouraged from traveling alone, told it's not safe, not practical, or not suitable.

But what if I told you that solo travel can be a transformative, liberating, and life-changing experience?

Within these pages, I'll show you that with the right mindset, preparation, and strategies, you can confidently explore the world on your own terms.

Solo travel requires you to step out of your comfort zone which, in turn, promotes personal growth & self-discovery. On top of that, you get the ultimate level of flexibility and spontaneity. You are in charge of the itinerary and you can make any changes you need to, without one word of complaint.

It can boost your confidence levels, knowing that you made this trip happen on your own and required little to no help. Without distractions, you can fully immerse yourself in local cultures and experiences. You have time to reflect and you don't have to make compromises. That is my favorite part about traveling alone: No one can say No!

Also, traveling alone isn't just about logistics—it's a mindset shift. It requires bravery, adaptability, and a willingness to challenge the boundaries of your comfort zone. And in return, it offers incredible rewards:

**Self-Discovery-** Without the influence of others, you truly get to know yourself—your likes, dislikes, and hidden strengths. Every decision is yours, and that autonomy is powerful.
**Unmatched Freedom-** You wake up when you want, linger at a museum for hours, switch up your itinerary on a whim—there's no compromising, no negotiating. Just pure flexibility.
**Confidence Boost-** Planning, navigating, and thriving in a new environment on your own is no small feat. Each experience builds resilience, proving you're capable of handling whatever comes your way.
**Cultural Immersion-** Solo travelers tend to engage more deeply with their surroundings. Without the distraction of familiar companions, you soak in the details—the sights, the

flavors, the conversations—and connect authentically with locals.

**Story Time:**

My first official solo trip was to Las Vegas. It wasn't glamorous or spontaneous—it was simply a trip I wanted to take for myself. In the past, I'd only been there for emergencies, barely scraping the surface of the city's magic. This time, I went for me.

I bundled my flight, hotel, and a three-day monorail pass, mapping out the perfect blend of structured activities and free exploration. As soon as I arrived, I changed into comfortable clothes, grabbed an over-sized slushie (because why not?), and hopped on a tour bus. The tour helped me to take mental notes of all the paces I planned to visit the following day.

My hotel provided two free buffets, So I didn't have to worry about meals whenever I found the time to eat. I wandered the famous Strip at my own pace, slipping into attractions that intrigued me, people-watching, and savoring the ability to decide exactly how I spent my time. The best part is that everything was paid for in advance, including, the hotel, airport shuttle, monorail and attractions, by bundling with Southwest Vacations, which I will expand on in another chapter.

And when the trip ended, I walked away feeling victorious. I had done this on my own. I had navigated an unfamiliar city, stayed safe, and enjoyed myself without a single compromise.

That trip changed everything. It wasn't just a getaway—it was proof that solo travel wasn't just possible; it was *empowering*. Since then, I've taken countless solo adventures, each one expanding my confidence and my view of the world.

Solo travel isn't reckless; it's revolutionary. It's proof that you can shape your own experiences without limitations, that the world is as open to you as it is to anyone else. It doesn't matter if you start small—a weekend getaway, a solo dinner date in a new city, a short road trip. The important part is that you begin. Because once you do, the question won't be "Should I travel alone?"—it'll be "Where should I go next?" And trust me, that's the best question to ask.

## { 2 }

# GIRLS TRIP, OR NAH?

There's a certain power in traveling together, and I firmly believe in strength in numbers. That's why I'm always open to a girl's trip—it's not just about sharing experiences, but also about looking out for one another. When exploring unfamiliar places, there can be unexpected dangers, and having a group of trusted companions provides an added layer of security. Whether it's navigating a new city, handling unexpected situations, or simply enjoying the adventure together, there's comfort in knowing that support is just a step away. Traveling with friends turns a simple getaway into something even more meaningful—it's about creating unforgettable memories while ensuring everyone's well-being.

Let's weigh some pros & cons of group travel.

**A few Pros:**

**Bonding and connection**: a girls' trip can strengthen friendships and create lifelong memories.

**Empowerment:** a chance to focus on yourself and your relationships with friends.

**Adventure and exploration:** try new experiences and explore new places together.

**Support and encouragement**: a safe space to share thoughts, feelings, and experiences.

**No judgments:** a safe space to be yourself without fear of criticism.

**A few Cons:**

**Cost:** travel and accommodation expenses can add up.

**Planning and organization:** coordinating schedules and activities can be challenging.

**Different personalities and interests:** conflicting opinions and preferences.

**Drama and conflict:** potential for disagreements and tension.

**Exhaustion:** packed itineraries and late nights can lead to burnout.

**Comparison and competition:** unhealthy comparisons or competitions within the group regarding money, status, etc.

Best practice is to ONLY travel with people you are close to. By exploring new cities with people you already know and love, you can skip the awkward getting-to-know-you phase and dive straight into shared adventures and laughter. With close friends, you can create personalized itineraries tailored to your group's interests and preferences and enjoy activities that resonate with everyone.

Traveling with close friends provides emotional support, inside jokes, and a sense of belonging, making even the most challenging moments enjoyable. Without the stress of navigating unfamiliar social dynamics, you can relax, be yourself, and fully immerse in the experience.

{ 3 }

# WRITING YOUR ITINERARY

Generating an itinerary for a trip is a crucial step in planning a successful and stress-free journey. It involves carefully curating a schedule of activities, destinations, and travel arrangements to maximize your time and enjoyment. Start by identifying your top priorities and interests, and then research the best times to visit each location. Consider factors like travel time, opening hours, and ticket requirements to ensure a smooth flow.

Be realistic about how much you can fit into each day, leaving room for spontaneity and flexibility. Use travel guides, apps, and websites to help organize your thoughts and create a visual timeline. Don't forget to include downtime and relaxation, as well as contingencies for unexpected changes or cancellations.

For group travel, let the most organized person type up the itinerary, provide a copy for everyone in the group and give them the opportunity to suggest changes.

**Story time:**

My first and only attempt at creating a group itinerary failed miserably (insert laughing emoji). It turned out, I was traveling across the country, from one beach state to another with 2 people who would rather stay up all night, sleep all day, and then lounge next to a hotel pool to take pictures, than to explore the beautiful city of Miami and take in the culture and amazing food.

Please be sure to ONLY travel with like-minded people. When writing an itinerary for either group or solo travel, you have 2 options: Daily itinerary, or Hourly itinerary.

Daily works best when the items on your to-do list don't have schedules. For instance, if you are driving from one town to the next, and only planning to visit public spaces, like parks and restaurants that don't require a reservation, a daily itinerary might be a good choice.

An Hourly itinerary works best for when you are visiting locations within a close proximity of each other, or when you have cruises, tours, shows etc. scheduled.

On my road trips between multiple states, I would write down the dates and then list the things I wanted to do and places I planned to visit each day.

When visiting a single city, I would write down the time I am setting my alarm for, the time I will have to shower and dress, the time I plan to eat, and the times I needed to be at each location. I even wrote down my bedtime. I wanted to make the most of every minute.

**See bonus section at the end of this guide for example itineraries.**

# { 4 }

# WHERE TO GO

Selecting a travel destination can indeed be the most challenging aspect of trip planning. And the thought of traveling alone can be both exciting and overwhelming. scary. But the thought of wasting years, waiting for the right guy to vacation with, or simply waiting for your friend's schedules to align with yours, can feel even worse.

This is the time to break out of your shell, leave your comfort zone and start your traveling journey! This guide will not only give you some safe, solo- traveling tips, but it can be used to plan and execute your next girl's trip.

First, think about the type of vacation you want to take. Are you looking for relaxation and beach time, or an action-packed adventure in the mountains? Do you want to explore vibrant cities, historic landmarks, or experience the great outdoors?

Identifying your priorities will help you focus on destinations that fit your vision. Consider the time of year and weather conditions. If you're looking for warm weather, destinations like Florida, California, or Hawaii might be ideal.

For a winter wonderland experience, head to Colorado, Utah, or Vermont. Spring and fall are great times to visit the Northeast, Southeast, or Pacific Northwest for mild temperatures and beautiful foliage.

Think about your budget and how far you're willing to travel. If you're on a tight budget, consider destinations within driving distance or opt for affordable cities like Portland, Maine, or Asheville, North Carolina.

If you're willing to splurge, look into luxury resorts in destinations like Napa Valley, California, or Jackson Hole, Wyoming. Culture and history buffs might enjoy destinations like New Orleans, Louisiana, with its rich jazz heritage and delicious Creole cuisine, or Boston, Massachusetts, with its Freedom Trail and world-class museums.

Nature lovers might prefer destinations like Yellowstone National Park, Yosemite National Park, or the Grand Canyon.

Foodies will find plenty of options to indulge in local cuisine, from seafood in Maine to barbecue in Texas, or wine tastings in Oregon.

Outdoor enthusiasts can explore the scenic beauty of Alaska, hike the Appalachian Trail, or kayak through the bioluminescent bay in Puerto Rico.

When choosing a destination, also consider the local vibe and atmosphere. Do you prefer a bustling city, a quaint small town, or a secluded natural setting?

Think about the activities and amenities you want to have access to, such as restaurants, shops, or entertainment options.

Reflect on places you've always dreamed of visiting. Perhaps there's a specific city, national park, or coastal town that has captured your imagination. Revisit locations where past experiences were less than ideal. Sometimes the right company—or lack thereof—can significantly impact our perception of a place.

It took me four visits to Las Vegas to truly appreciate its allure. Interestingly, it was during my first solo trip that I finally connected with the city. As a solo traveler, I immersed myself in the tourist experience, explored various attractions, and even had the unexpected pleasure of meeting Sigfried (of Sigfried & Roy) in person.

If you're unsure of your dream destination, a quick Google search of popular U.S. attractions can provide inspiration.

Some of the most popular domestic destinations include:
1. **Glacier National Park, Montana**
2. **Maui, Hawaii**
3. **Grand Canyon National Park, Arizona**
4. **New York City, New York**
5. **San Francisco, California**
6. **Washington, D.C.**
7. **Key West, Florida**
8. **San Diego, California**
9. **Yellowstone National Park, Wyoming**
10. **New Orleans, Louisiana**

Whether you're drawn to natural wonders, cultural hubs, or historical landmarks, as long as it is affordable, don't be afraid to take the plunge.

It also doesn't hurt to travel to the next state over just to see what it has to offer. This also makes for a great weekend trip. Not all vacations have to last an entire week.

Use this space to write down your top destinations. Be sure to use pencil so you can erase and update if necessary.

---------------------------------------------------
---------------------------------------------------
---------------------------------------------------
---------------------------------------------------
---------------------------------------------------
---------------------------------------------------
---------------------------------------------------
---------------------------------------------------
---------------------------------------------------
---------------------------------------------------
---------------------------------------------------
---------------------------------------------------

Wanna visit a tropical Paradise without leaving the USA? Consider these Destinations:

**Puerto Rico**

**US Virgin Islands**
**Guam**
**American Samoa.**

These destinations only require valid I.D. and some require a valid Birth Certificate.

Considering a Cruise? These (round-trip) destinations usually don't require a passport, but it's a good idea to bring it anyway:

**Bermuda**
**Dominican Republic**
**British Virgin Islands**
**The Bahamas**
**Jamaica**
**Costa Rica**
**St. Martin**
**The Cayman Islands**
**Honduras** & more.

Some parts of Mexico and Canada are accessible without a passport, on a cruise. Just remember to do your research before booking.

**In the next two chapters, I will give you all my best tips for saving money on travel and transportation.**

> *"To awaken quite alone in a strange town is one of the pleasantest sensations in the world."* – Freya Stark

## { 5 }

# FUNDING YOUR TRIP

*"Invest in experiences; they pay the best dividends."* -Unknown

Wondering if you can afford to travel? I have some tips that may help!

> (Driving? See Chapters: Transportation & Utilize Daylight Hours.)

If you have already save up the money for a trip, you can save these tips for later, or use them to stretch your savings:

**Create a Dedicated Savings Plan-** Set aside a specific amount each month by opening a separate vacation fund account. Automating your savings ensures that funds don't inadvertently get spent on daily expenses. Whether you start with a small contribution or a substantial chunk, watching that account gradually fill up can be incredibly motivating as you see your travel fund grow. This dedicated approach helps make your vacation a deliberate financial goal rather than a spontaneous splurge.

**Budget and Prioritize-** Examine your monthly expenses and decide which items are essentials and which can be trimmed. By assigning a fixed percentage of your income to vacation expenses, you create a clear priority system. This process might involve cutting back on non-essential spending like expensive dinners or impulse purchases, but it paves the way for investing in experiences that enrich your life. Over time, prioritizing your travel fund becomes a rewarding habit.

**Use Travel Rewards Credit Cards-** Daily purchases can quickly add up—and if you're using the right credit card, they can also add to your travel rewards. Earn points or miles every time you shop, dine out, or even fill up your gas tank. Just remember to pay off your balance each month to avoid interest charges. Over time, these rewards can be redeemed for flights, hotel stays, or even entire vacation packages, turning everyday spending into an investment in your future adventures.

**Take Advantage of Sales and Discounts**- Booking flights, hotels, and vacation packages during off-peak seasons or promotional periods can lead to significant savings. It helps to subscribe to travel newsletters, follow deal sites, or set up notifications from your favorite travel apps. Being flexible with your travel dates often leads to better prices, allowing you to stretch your vacation budget further while still enjoying premium experiences.

**Consider a Side Hustle**- Boosting your travel fund doesn't always mean cutting costs—it can also mean increasing your income. A part-time job, freelance work, or even monetizing a hobby can provide additional funds for your vacation. Side hustles not only offer financial rewards but also add a creative and fulfilling challenge to your routine, making your journey towards your dream trip even more satisfying.

**Use Cashback and Travel Apps**- Digital tools like Rakuten®, Ebates®, or Hopper® help you keep more money in your pocket. These apps give cashback on everyday purchases or alert you to discounts on flights and accommodations. With a little extra savings from these tools, you might feel more confident about splurging on that extra day of sightseeing or a memorable dining experience abroad.

**Plan Ahead**- Booking accommodations and flights well in advance can secure you much better rates. Early planning gives you a wider selection of travel dates and lodging options, often translating to significant savings. Plus, having your travel details sorted out ahead of time transforms your vacation from a rushed decision into a well-organized, exciting journey where you can focus on the experiences ahead rather than last-minute logistics.

**Use Travel Loans or Financing Options**- For some, waiting to save enough might dampen the excitement. In such cases, exploring reputable travel loans or financing options can be a practical solution. However, always pay close attention to the interest rates and repayment terms. Responsible borrowing for travel can be worthwhile if it doesn't compromise your long-term financial well-being.

**Crowdfunding**- Crowdfunding isn't just for startups—it can also work for travel plans, especially if your trip has a unique theme or purpose. Sharing your vacation plans with friends and family might inspire contributions toward your journey. Often, people enjoy being a part of your adventure just as much as you do, and their support—monetary or otherwise—can add a special layer of connection to your trip.

**Sell Unwanted Items**- De-cluttering your space not only creates room for new memories but can also generate extra cash to fund your travels. Whether it's selling gently used clothes online or having a garage sale, turning unwanted items into cash can boost your vacation budget without extra work or earning a side income long term.

**Use Travel Agencies or Consolidators**- Travel agencies and consolidators often offer exclusive package deals, discounts, or bundled offers that might be hard to find on your own. They have insider access to discounts with airlines, hotels, and rental car services, enabling you to enjoy significant savings. This can be a particularly good option if you're planning a multi-destination trip.

**Use Budgeting Tools**- Apps like Mint® or Personal Capital® are invaluable for tracking your expenses and keeping a close eye on your incoming funds. By monitoring your spending habits in real-time, you can adjust your budget to ensure that you're steadily building your vacation fund. These tools provide clear insights into your financial health, making it easier to balance your travel dreams with everyday expenses.

**Prioritize Experiences Over Material Possessions**- Ultimately, vacation memories are far more valuable than material possessions. Instead of splurging on the latest gadgets or trendy fashion, consider investing in once-in-a-lifetime experiences. Whether it's a guided tour, an adventurous excursion, or a culinary class abroad, focusing on experiences enriches your life, creates lasting memories, and aligns your expenditures with your values.

Remember:

No matter how excited you are about your next adventure, always prioritize your overall financial health. Ensure you have an emergency fund in place and that your essential financial responsibilities are met before channeling funds into travel. A balanced approach means you can enjoy your vacation now without compromising your future.

These strategies not only empower you to finance your vacation but also encourage you to adopt healthier financial habits. What aspect of vacation planning do you find most challenging—saving, budgeting, or finding the best deals? Perhaps you have other creative ideas you swear by; I'd love to hear more about your travel money hacks or the next destination on your bucket list!

## *PLANE TICKETS*

When it comes to searching for airline tickets, my top resource is Google Flights®. This powerful tool allows you to view every flight available to your desired destination from your chosen airport, all within the specific date and time range you prefer. It provides a comprehensive, side-by-side comparison of flight options, highlighting the best routes with the shortest travel times and the lowest prices. By aggregating flight data in one convenient location, it transforms a potentially overwhelming decision into a streamlined process, giving travelers the clarity they need to make informed choices.

A recent and exciting update is the inclusion of Southwest Airlines® on Google Flights®. After a period of being excluded, Southwest has made its return, which means you can now compare its fares alongside other carriers directly from this platform. Even though Southwest is now visible on Google Flights®, it's worth visiting Southwest.com to tap into their 'Low Fare Calendar.' This special feature displays the lowest price available for each day of the month, giving you a clear picture of the most cost-effective travel dates, and ensuring you never miss a deal.

Southwest Airlines was well known for allowing two free checked bags on every flight, which significantly cut down on travel expenses if you're carrying extra luggage. But their policy recently changed.

Their flexible payment options are still a highlight; you can pay with points, cash, or even opt for monthly installments through Uplift®, provided you have qualified credit. This means you can manage your travel budget better while still enjoying the benefits associated with flying Southwest.

If you need additional flexibility with your travel payments, there are alternative financing options available. Affirm® is one service featured on Southwest.com that allows you to split your payment into manageable monthly installments or four bi-weekly payments depending on the amount. Beyond that, services like Zip Pay® provide the ability to create a virtual credit card that works with any website accepting card payments. With Zip Pay®, you also have the option to make four bi-weekly payments, further easing the financial load of booking your next adventure.

For many travelers, bundling your vacation components is an appealing way to manage costs and simplify planning. Southwest Vacations® is one of my favorite tools for this purpose. It allows you to bundle not just your flight, but also hotels, car rentals, and even attractions at select destinations. The option to include round-trip transportation to and from the airport adds yet another layer of convenience. Priceline® offers a similar bundling service, and its VIP tiers—accumulated quickly with regular use—open the door to additional discounts on not only lodging but also flights and rental cars.

If your travels involve flying with Delta®, the opportunity to earn miles is another thread in your travel savings strategy. By signing up with partners such as Lyft®—though this offer is available for a limited time—and Starbucks®, you transform everyday spending into valuable Delta Airline® miles. Visit deltastarbucks.com for more information. Each dollar spent through their dedicated platforms or on Delta Skymiles Shopping® contributes to your flight mileage. This means that even routine purchases help you inch closer to your next upgrade or free flight.

Finally, while every traveler's priorities differ, it's important to remember that flights are simply a means of getting from point A to point B. Though first-class travel might appeal to those looking for a splurge experience, I personally see great value in flying coach. Choosing the more economical option not only allows you to save money but also frees up extra funds for spending on memorable experiences at your destination. Whether it's an upgrade or sticking to the basics, every decision can enhance your overall journey—ensuring that your travel remains both enjoyable and financially sensible.

**Ask Yourself These Questions:**

1. What is My Budget?
2. How Long Can I Travel?
3. What Type of Travel Do I Enjoy?
4. What Are My Priorities?
5. What Are My Must-See Destinations?
6. Solo or Group Travel?
7. Does My Job Offer Rewards Such as Discounts on Travel/ Attractions?

*"The world is a book, and those who do not travel read only a page."*
 -Saint Augustine

# { 6 }

# LODGING

If you are traveling solo, I would recommend avoiding Hostels and shared Lodging.

One solid option is Airbnb®. The platform stands out because it displays the full price—complete with all fees—up front. This transparency helps you plan your budget more accurately and makes it easier to choose a space that fits your comfort level and needs. The reviews and host profiles available on the app also provide an added layer of trust, allowing you to select accommodations that have been vetted by previous guests.

Another excellent resource is Priceline®. I personally favor this app because it offers a rewards program with several VIP tiers that accumulate benefits from January to December, extending into the following year. These tiers offer not just discounts on hotels, but also on rental cars and additional travel essentials. An appealing feature of Priceline® is its route-based search, which shows you all available lodging along your current travel path. This can be incredibly useful if you're mapping out your journey and want flexibility in where you stay next.

### Choosing the Right Hotel

When it comes to selecting a hotel, thorough research and attention to detail can make all the difference. Here's a checklist to guide you:

-Look for accommodations that offer free Wi-Fi, complimentary breakfast, and—most importantly—free parking. These amenities can greatly reduce your daily expenses while traveling and boost your overall convenience.

-Read guest reviews and research the area's safety ratings. Tools like Google Maps Street View enable you to virtually navigate the neighborhood to spot nearby conveniences such as restaurants, convenience stores, and pharmacies. This preemptive check can save you from late-night drives or feeling isolated in an unfamiliar location.

-Choose hotels with 24-hour front desks and security personnel.

-Ensure that entrances, hallways, and common areas are well lit and regularly monitored.

-Avoid leaving sensitive documents (like your passport) out in the open; store them safely.

-Always keep an eye on your belongings in common areas and avoid leaving your bags unattended, even for a short time.
   -Save emergency numbers in your phone, including local police and the hotel front desk.
   -A personal safety whistle or an alarm can be a great tool to alert others if you ever feel threatened.

   By conducting careful research and choosing accommodations with robust security measures, you set the stage for a more relaxed and enjoyable travel experience.

   Once you secure a lodging arrangement, the next step is ensuring your immediate physical safety. When you arrive at your lodging, take a moment to assess the area. In the parking lot, note if there are ample security measures such as good lighting and visible surveillance cameras. Once you enter the lobby, remain observant. If you notice that your room number is being announced loudly by the attendant—even in passing—politely request that they refrain from doing so or ask for an alternative room. Such small actions can prevent unwarranted attention from individuals who might be lingering around.

If you have to take an elevator to your room floor, try to wait until you can ride alone. While it might seem like a minor detail, riding solo in an elevator minimizes the chance of unwanted interactions and gives you a moment of privacy as you transition to your room.

Once you enter your room, immediately close and latch the door. Double-check that any additional security features, such as a deadbolt or chain latch, are properly engaged. This simple step reinforces your personal safety and ensures that your room remains a private haven during your stay.

Remember, your safety is a priority. By following these precautions, you can enjoy your travels while staying secure in your hotel room.

Ultimately, the key to solo travel is striking a balance between adventure and caution. While these measures might seem meticulous, they are essential for ensuring that your journey is as safe as it is enriching. Trust your instincts—if something doesn't feel right, take immediate action, whether that means requesting a room change or dialing a trusted contact.

*"Travel only with thy equals or thy betters; if there are none, travel alone."*

– The Dhammapada

# { 7 }

# TRANSPORTATION

Once you reach your destination, you're going to need to get around. If you're visiting a walk-able town and don't need transportation you've hit the jackpot! If not, here are some tips for getting around.

### *ROAD TRIP*

If you decide to drive to your destination, make sure to Prepare Your Vehicle in Advance:

**Check Fluid Levels**: Ensure your oil, coolant, and other fluids are at the right levels.

**Inspect Tires**: Check tire tread and pressure. Carry a spare tire and necessary tools.

**Test Lights and Wipers**: Ensure all lights are functional, and wipers work well.

**Gas Up Before Departure**: Fill up your tank to avoid higher prices on highways. Try using the 'Gas Buddy'® app to find the lowest gas price in your area. It constantly updated by local app users so it can be pretty accurate.

**Insurance Coverage**: Verify your insurance coverage for roadside assistance and emergencies and find out if those services are available in other states.

**Avoid Hitchhikers:** While the idea of helping someone in need may seem noble, picking up hitchhikers can come with serious risks. You never truly know a stranger's intentions, and inviting an unknown individual into your vehicle could lead to dangerous situations. Some hitchhikers may be genuinely in need, but others could have ulterior motives, putting both your safety and belongings at risk.

If you ever feel compelled to assist someone on the road, consider calling local authorities or roadside assistance rather than offering a ride. Trusting your instincts is key—if a situation feels off, it's best to prioritize your safety. When traveling, always remain vigilant, keep your doors locked, and avoid unnecessary risks that could put you in a vulnerable position. Staying cautious can help ensure your journey remains both safe and enjoyable.

## REST AREAS

As a solo traveler, rest stops can be a convenient and necessary break during long road trips. However, it's essential to prioritize your safety while stopping at these areas. When pulling into a rest stop, choose a well-lit and populated area, avoiding isolated or dark parking spots. Keep your doors and windows locked and be cautious of your surroundings.

When exiting your vehicle, take note of your belongings and keep valuables out of sight. Avoid leaving your car unattended for extended periods, as this can attract unwanted attention. If you need to use the restroom or stretch your legs, try to do so quickly and stay alert. Be mindful of strangers approaching you or your vehicle and trust your instincts if a situation feels uncomfortable.

Additionally, consider the time of day and avoid
stopping at rest stops during late-night or early- morning hours when they may be less populated. If possible, stop at rest stops near major highways or interstates, as these tend to have more surveillance and foot traffic. Keep your phone charged and easily accessible in case of an emergency.

Finally, be prepared and aware of your surroundings. Keep a roadside emergency kit in your car, including items like a flashlight, first aid kit, and snacks. If you feel uncomfortable or sense danger, don't hesitate to leave the rest stop and seek a safer location. By being proactive and taking necessary precautions, you can minimize risks and ensure a safe and enjoyable journey.

## *RENTAL CAR*

Whether you rent a car to drive to your destination or rent one at the airport in your destination city, you'll want to make sure you're getting the best deal. Opt for an economy car whenever possible. If you're traveling in a group, a larger car might be a better fit.

Utilize the Priceline® app and your VIP status for car rentals. All car rental companies offer additional insurance coverage, but Priceline offers their own insurance for a small daily fee. If you want to be sure your rental is fully covered for any possible damage, I suggest opting for the insurance in the app.

I have had great experiences with Alamo® and Hertz®. Alamo® gives a reduced Incidentals hold if you can show a return ticket back to where you're visiting from. Hertz's ®Gold membership provides a seamless experience from check out to check in.

Be sure to rent vehicles that offer unlimited miles if you plan to use it for a road trip. Keep in mind,

that there may be extra charges if you pick up from one location and drop off at another. Ask in advance.

**Here are some tips for driving in a new city:**

## PLAN AHEAD

**Research Routes**: Familiarize yourself with the city's major roads, highways, and traffic patterns before you hit the road. Google Maps® allows you to view images of the route step by step.

**GPS or Navigation Apps**: Use a reliable GPS or navigation app to guide you. Set it up before you start driving to avoid distractions.

STAY ALERT!

**Mind the Speed Limits**: Pay attention to posted speed limits, especially in residential areas and school zones as they may be slightly different.

**Avoid Distractions**: Put away your phone and focus on driving. City driving requires constant attention.

**Anticipate Aggressive Drivers**: Some city drivers can be impatient. Stay calm and avoid confrontations.

**Toll Roads**: Be prepared for tolls and understand the payment methods. Try researching the Toll companies in your destination city.

## PARKING

**Find Safe Parking**: Look for well-lit, secure parking lots or garages. Avoid leaving valuables visible in your car.

**Check Parking Signs**: Read parking signs carefully to avoid tickets or towing. Some cities have strict rules about street parking.

## TRAIN RIDES

Taking a train to your vacation destination offers a unique and rewarding travel experience. Not only can it be a more environmentally friendly option compared to flying or driving, but it also allows you to unwind and enjoy the scenic views along the way.

Without the hassle of traffic or security lines, you can relax in comfort and stretch your legs freely. Many trains also offer amenities like food and beverage services, electrical outlets, and Wi-Fi.

Additionally, trains often arrive in the heart of cities, making it easy to access your accommodation and start exploring.

The train is best utilized for short distances (San Francisco to Seattle, for instance).

If you don't plan to be on the train for more than a day, the cost may be a lot lower than if you were going cross country. You may be able to request a private room so you can lie down when you need to sleep.

## LONG DISTANCE BUS RIDES

If you want to save money, have plenty of time, have a fear of flying, or don't like moving at high speeds, consider taking a ride on a Greyhound® or Flix bus®. Greyhound® can take you across the country in about three days. Flixbus® is a cheap alternative for shorter trips.

**Ask Bus and Train companies if they offer group rates for your girls' trip.**

### *PUBLIC TRANSPORTATION*

Using public transportation while traveling is a cost-effective way to explore a new destination without breaking the bank. By utilizing the buses, trains, and subways instead of taxis or rental cars, you can save a significant amount of money on transportation costs.

Additionally, public transportation often provides a unique perspective on the local culture and daily life, allowing you to blend in with commuters and experience the city like a local.

With a little planning and research, you can navigate public transportation systems with ease, and use the money you save to indulge in local cuisine, attractions, and activities that make your trip truly unforgettable.

Plus, you may be able to see some new places that were not on your list of places to visit.

If you are visiting New Orleans, the streetcar is a great option. Try searching for hotels along the streetcar route so you can limit the amount of walking you will have to do after a long day of exploring. It also makes for safer traveling so there is less of a chance of someone following you back to your hotel.

(See 'Listen to Your Gut!' Chapter)

The streetcar travels to some of the most popular tourist destinations, which can save you a ton of money on Taxi Services.

Google® will always let you know if there is public transportation available to get you where you need to go. Simply open the Google Maps app, enter your destination, then choose the public transit icon.

Most public transportation companies offer daily or weekly passes which can save money overall. Check Google® for local transportation websites and apps.

"The adventure begins when you step onto the bus."
-Unknown

## { 8 }

# CRUISING BABES

Finding the perfect cruise accommodations can seem slightly intimidating, but websites like southwestcruises.com and cruises.com offer the simplest way to build an itinerary from start to finish.

For the solo woman or a group of adventurous women, a cruise offers an undeniable blend of freedom, security, and empowerment. Cruising transforms travel into a celebration of independence while fostering an environment where you can connect with like-minded women from around the globe.

Every wave that carries you from one destination to the next becomes a reminder that you are charting your own course—a journey that is as much about self-discovery as it is about exploration. Within the safety and comfort of a modern cruise ship, you have the opportunity to escape the everyday, invest in truly memorable experiences, and form meaningful connections that can last a lifetime.

Onboard, the ship transforms into a dynamic space where every detail has been designed to cater to diverse interests and tastes. Whether you're looking to unwind with a soothing spa treatment, participate in vibrant dance classes, or engage in creative workshops designed specifically for women travelers, there is a welcoming social scene waiting for you.

The secure, inclusive environment of a cruise ship allows you the freedom to explore your passions and indulge in moments of self-care at your own pace.

Evenings are filled with live entertainment, ranging from musical performances and comedy shows to engaging talks and themed parties that celebrate the spirit of sisterhood. The all-in-one nature of a cruise means that travel logistics are taken care of, letting you focus on what truly matters—enjoying each precious moment.

The versatility of cruising extends well beyond the ship's decks. Each port of call offers new avenues to immerse yourself in the local culture while maintaining the reassurance of a structured, group-friendly environment. Onshore excursions provide a chance to explore historic sites, bustling local markets, and pristine natural landscapes. Many of these itineraries can be tailored to suit a women's travel group, ensuring that you experience destinations on guided tours led by knowledgeable, sometimes female, experts. Whether you opt for a budget-friendly adventure or are inclined to splurge on an exclusive guided tour or a private culinary class featuring local delicacies, the options allow you to craft an itinerary that aligns perfectly with your desires and financial plan.

While cruising offers a myriad of complimentary activities, there are also premium experiences available for those moments when you want to treat yourself. Investing in a gourmet dining experience or a signature spa treatment may come at a higher cost, but these elevated privileges often enhance your voyage with indulgence and personalized care. The decision to splurge on these special activities should be viewed as an investment in unforgettable memories and moments of luxury—a balance between everyday enjoyment and those rare, exquisite experiences that remind you of your own strength and worth.

For solo travelers, cruising provides a particularly reassuring framework. The camaraderie of a group of women, whether traveling together or simply joining a community of fellow female explorers on board, creates an atmosphere where safety and empowerment go hand in hand. Navigating unfamiliar ports becomes less daunting when you're surrounded by peers who share your love of adventure, and the organized excursions, secure amenities, and attentive staff ensure that every step of your journey is as safe as it is spirited. This well-rounded blend of independence and collective support is what makes cruising such an attractive option for women seeking both self-reliance and connection.

Ultimately, embarking on a cruise as a solo woman or as part of a group of women is more than just a vacation—it's a powerful affirmation of your right to explore the world on your own terms. From the exhilarating onboard activities to the carefully curated shore excursions, each moment at sea serves as a testament to your courage, independence, and the endless possibilities that lie ahead. Embrace the rhythm of the ocean, celebrate the vibrant tapestry of cultures waiting at every port, and let your journey be enriched by the shared experiences and lifelong friendships that are forged along the way. Your voyage is a story waiting to be written—a narrative of empowerment, discovery, and the joy of living fully in every sunrise and sunset.

{ 9 }

# EXPAND YOUR HORIZONS

Have you chosen a destination city or state yet? Chances are, you've opted for a major city—after all, each state has several that offer unique attractions, rich history, and vibrant cultures. But have you considered broadening your itinerary and visiting multiple cities within one trip? If you're embarking on a road trip or renting a vehicle with unlimited mileage, driving to nearby destinations can be a fantastic way to maximize your adventure while ensuring you make it back in time for your return flight.

One of my travel goals has been to visit at least one major city in every state, and lately, I've found myself gravitating toward neighboring states to explore their closest major cities. For example, in 2022, I flew into Portland, Oregon, then drove up to Seattle, Washington, before making my way south to Springfield and Eugene, Oregon. Later that year, I flew into San Jose, California, then took a short drive up to San Francisco, then down along the stunning Big Sur coastline.

The summer of 2024 was especially exciting—I traveled with my daughter, flying into Salt Lake City, Utah, before road-tripping through Idaho, Montana, and Wyoming. By the end of the trip, we had colored in four states on the US Map!

While these multi-city adventures have been exhilarating, some stretches kept me on the road for up to six hours each day. That's why it's important to choose destinations that match your driving comfort level. Long hours on the road can be tiring, so planning scenic routes, factoring in rest stops, and ensuring you have enjoyable detours can make the journey more rewarding. If you're up for an unforgettable adventure, consider mapping out multiple destinations—you'll see more, experience more, and create lifelong memories along the way.

*"No matter how far a person can go the horizon is still way beyond you."*

—Zora Neale Hurston

… { 10 }

# RECOGNIZE TOURIST TRAPS

To avoid tourist traps, it's essential to research your destination thoroughly before arriving. Look for reviews and recommendations from trusted sources, such as travel blogs, forums, and guidebooks. Be wary of overly promotional or biased information, and instead, opt for authentic and balanced perspectives.

Another way to avoid tourist traps is to venture off the beaten path. Instead of sticking to popular tourist areas, explore local neighborhoods and hidden gems that are often overlooked by visitors. This will not only help you avoid crowds and overpriced attractions but also give you a more authentic taste of the local culture.

Be cautious of attractions or activities that seem too good to be true or are heavily promoted by locals. These are often tourist traps designed to part you from your money.

Instead, ask locals for recommendations or seek out smaller, family-owned businesses that offer more genuine experiences.

Additionally, be mindful of your surroundings and trust your instincts. If an area or attraction feels overly commercialized or suspicious, it's best to avoid it. Keep an eye out for red flags such as inflated prices, aggressive sales tactics, or low-quality goods and services.

To further avoid tourist traps, consider visiting popular attractions during off-peak hours or seasons. This will help you avoid crowds and long lines, and often, you'll find better deals and more relaxed atmospheres. Also, be open to trying local transportation, such as public buses or trains, instead of relying on touristy shuttles or taxis.

Finally, remember that it's okay to say no to attractions or activities that don't interest you or seem like tourist traps. Prioritize your own preferences and budget, and don't feel pressured to participate in something that doesn't feel right. By being informed, adventurous, and discerning, you can avoid tourist traps and have a more enjoyable and authentic travel experience.

**Examples of Tourist Traps:**

1. Overpriced restaurants or bars in popular tourist areas, often with mediocre food and drink quality.
2. Street performers or artists who demand money for photos or interactions.
3. "Discount" shops or markets selling low-quality or counterfeit goods at inflated prices.
4. Guided tours that promise exclusive access or experiences but deliver generic or superficial information.
5. "Must-see" attractions or museums with excessive entrance fees or long lines.
6. Aggressive vendors or salespeople pushing overpriced souvenirs or services.
7. "Authentic" cultural experiences that feel staged or artificial, such as fake traditional villages or performances.
8. High-priced transportation services, like taxi scams or overpriced shuttle buses.
9. Timeshare or vacation club presentations disguised as free tours or gifts.
10. Photo opportunities with "local" characters or props that demand tips or payment.
11. Overpriced and low-quality accommodations, such as hostels or hotels with poor conditions.

12. Tourist-friendly "local" restaurants serving bland or adapted versions of traditional cuisine. Remember, it's essential to research and stay informed to avoid these tourist traps and have a more authentic travel experience.

*The average tourist wants to go to places where there are no tourists."*
-Sam Ewing

## { 11 }

# UTILIZE DAYLIGHT HOURS

Maximizing your use of daylight hours while on vacation can truly transform the quality of your travel experience. Embracing the day allows you to immerse yourself in a rich tapestry of attractions, outdoor adventures, and cultural experiences that might otherwise go unnoticed. When you greet the morning by waking up early and witnessing the gentle glow of sunrise, you not only secure a head start but also open your eyes to the subtle beauty of a city or countryside awakened by gentle light. This peaceful start sets the tone for the rest of the day, inviting you to explore everything from bustling parks and serene beaches to scenic hiking trails that truly come alive when bathed in natural light.

Planning your itinerary ahead of time and choosing activities that benefit from daylight can help you ensure that each moment of your vacation is optimized for enjoyment. Many local events—whether vibrant markets, colorful festivals, or lively parades—are scheduled during the day, thus providing opportunities to engage meaningfully with the community and sample local traditions firsthand. Such experiences are not only memorable; they bring you closer to the cultural heartbeat of your destination and offer avenues for authentic interaction with locals, whose stories and customs enrich your travel narrative.

Beyond cultural enrichment, relying on daylight for your travel activities carries an inherent practicality, particularly in terms of safety. Tourist attractions, public transportation, and even the city's basic infrastructure tend to operate most efficiently during day hours. Navigating unfamiliar locales becomes far easier and more secure when every street is well-lit and life moves at a pace that's both visible and predictable. Relying on daytime travel can significantly reduce the uncertainties and potential risks that are more prominent after dark.

During a four-day road trip taken in the summer of 2024 with my daughter, the sunsets across the four states were as late as 9:00 pm, so we deliberately scheduled our driving and sightseeing activities to wind down by 8:00 pm, ensuring we were comfortably inside our hotel by 8:30 pm. This approach stemmed from a conscious decision to avoid the challenges and risks associated with driving in the dark, especially in cities we were just beginning to familiarize ourselves with. It was an effective strategy that not only boosted our day-to-day safety but also allowed us to fully appreciate the vibrancy of the daylight hours.

For solo travelers or those journeying with young children, the prudence of sticking to daytime exploration becomes even more significant. Late-night outings can introduce complexities and potential hazards, particularly in urban environments where reduced visibility can facilitate criminal activity. While the allure of discovering a city's nightlife is undeniable, the added comfort of group travel in those environments can provide much-needed security. If the nighttime ambiance intrigues you, consider experiencing it on a return trip with a group rather than venturing out alone.

In essence, capitalizing on daylight not only broadens your window for discovering new experiences but also integrates seamlessly with a mindset geared towards safety and thoughtful planning. It encourages you to structure your day so that every stop, every encounter, and every adventure unfolds in the clarity and security that only the sunlit hours can provide. As you make the most of each day under the light, you set the stage for creating lasting memories, confident in the knowledge that when night does fall, you've already woven a rich tapestry of experiences.

See next Chapter for Tips about Nightlife Safety.

*"As the sun dipped below the horizon, our journey found its sanctuary." - Unknown*

List some places to go with your girlfriends on a future trip:

---------------------------------------------------
---------------------------------------------------
---------------------------------------------------
---------------------------------------------------
---------------------------------------------------
---------------------------------------------------
---------------------------------------------------
-----------------------------------------

## { 12 }

# LISTEN TO YOUR GUT!

Prioritize safety over politeness. If something feels off, trust your instincts and act accordingly. Your gut rarely lets you down. If a situation feels uncomfortable, it probably is. Stay Aware and Lessen Vulnerability. Assume positivity, but don't assume everyone is friendly. Stay aware of your surroundings.

Inform someone you trust about your travel plans. Check in with them periodically.

> See 'Share Your Location' Chapter.

Avoid Excessive Alcohol. Enjoy drinks responsibly. Excessive alcohol impairs judgment and makes you vulnerable.

Stay Confident and Assertive. Walk with Purpose: Project confidence when walking alone. Avoid looking lost or unsure.

**Story time:** As I made my way back to the streetcar station in New Orleans, I couldn't help but notice a man walking a short distance ahead of me, repeatedly glancing over his shoulder in my direction. I was carrying a purse on my shoulder and had a slight limp due to the discomfort from my leather sandals. While my ego might have suggested that he was simply admiring me, my intuition was screaming warning signals, hinting at a more ominous intention.

He suddenly ducked into a doorway. As I approached the spot where the man had disappeared, he suddenly reappeared, peeking out from a doorway to wait for me to pass by. Unsettled by this, I quickly jaywalked across the street and sought refuge by striking up a conversation with a restaurant hostess, discreetly informing her that I was being followed.

She promptly offered me a warm hug, thanked me for being cautious, and invited me to wait inside for a few minutes until the coast was clear. Glancing across the street, I spotted a crowd gathering at the station, so I decided to walk in the opposite direction, joining the crowd just as the streetcar arrived. Feeling safer among the crowd of people, I boarded the streetcar, and the man stared me down until I was out of view.

If I hadn't been paying attention, I could have been robbed, or worse.

## STAY VIGILANT WHILE TRAVELING

**On The Road:**

While on the road, be mindful of your surroundings, especially at rest stops and gas stations. Avoid traveling alone at night and keep your doors and windows locked. If you need to stop, choose well-lit and populated areas, and consider using a buddy system if possible.

Consider using a personal safety app which allows you to quickly alert friends and family in case of an emergency.

**On Long Distance Train/ Bus Rides:**

When traveling by bus or train, Choose a seat in a well-lit and populated area, such as near the driver or in the middle of the train car. Avoid sitting alone in isolated areas or near suspicious individuals.

Keep your belongings close and secure, using a money belt or a secure bag. Consider using a luggage locker or storage compartment to keep your bags safe. Additionally, be mindful of your personal belongings, especially in crowded stations or terminals. To further enhance safety, consider sharing your itinerary with a friend or family member.

Be cautious when interacting with strangers, and avoid displaying signs of wealth (e.g., expensive jewelry or watches). If you feel uncomfortable or threatened, don't hesitate to alert the driver, conductor, or station staff. Many bus and train companies also offer safety measures such as security cameras and emergency alarms, so be aware of these resources in case of an emergency.

### On Flights & In Airports:

Before the flight, research the airline's safety record and policies regarding solo female travelers. Consider booking a direct flight to minimize layovers and connections.

Additionally, keep your valuables secure and be mindful of your belongings, especially in crowded airports.
During the flight, be aware of your surroundings and trust your instincts. If you feel uncomfortable or harassed

by a fellow passenger, don't hesitate to alert the flight attendants. They are trained to handle such situations and can re-seat you if necessary.

Many airlines also offer safety measures such as in-flight security cameras and emergency call buttons, so be aware of these resources in case of an emergency.

**On Cruise Ships:**

Familiarize yourself with the ship's safety features, such as the location of emergency exits, lifeboats, and security cameras. Attend the mandatory safety drill before the ship sets sail to understand evacuation procedures.

Additionally, be mindful of your surroundings, especially in crowded areas like bars and nightclubs. Avoid walking alone in isolated areas of the ship and consider using the ship's buddy system or joining a group tour to explore ports of call.

To further enhance safety, keep your cabin door locked and secure, and use the ship's safe to store valuables. Be cautious when meeting new people, and don't feel pressured to reveal personal information or accept drinks from strangers. If you feel uncomfortable or harassed, report incidents to ship security or a trusted crew member immediately.

Many cruise lines also offer safety measures such as 24-hour security patrols, emergency response plans, and counseling services, so be aware of these resources in case of an emergency.

**Keep your phone charged and accessible and consider sharing your flight itinerary with a friend or family member.**

## NIGHT LIFE

*The buddy system means watching each other's backs. Stay aware of your buddy's well-being, especially if alcohol is involved.*

Use the Buddy System if you decide to indulge in a night out with your friend group. There is strength in numbers! Whether you're hitting the local nightlife or exploring a vibrant festival, having a buddy significantly enhances safety. If your night out involves alcohol, designate a sober driver in advance. This could be someone in your group or a hired service, such as Uber or Lyft.

If you are traveling with friends, take turns being the designated driver. It is a fair way to ensure everyone enjoys the night without compromising safety.

**NEVER get behind the wheel if you have been drinking. Use ridesharing apps or walk back to your accommodation. Your safety—and that of others—depends on it!**

I don't recommend a night out on the town for solo travelers. Nightclubs can be crowded and chaotic, especially in unfamiliar cities. As a solo traveler, your safety is paramount. Without friends or companions, there is no one to watch your back. You are solely responsible for your safety.

If you encounter trouble, there's no immediate support system. Unfortunately, some nightclubs attract individuals with ill intentions. Solo women travelers are particularly vulnerable.

Watch out for unwanted attention, aggressive behavior, or attempts to isolate you.

### Be AWARE OF Human Trafficking

Human trafficking doesn't only happen abroad. Unfortunately, it is a major problem here in the United States.

Here are some ways to recognize and avoid human traffickers while on vacation:

-Be aware of overly friendly or flirtatious strangers who show unusual interest in your travel plans or personal life.

-Watch for individuals who offer unsolicited assistance or transportation, especially if they seem overly persistent.

-Be cautious of people who ask invasive questions about your financial situation, accommodation, or travel companions.

-Notice if someone is taking an unusual number of photos or videos of you, especially if they're focusing on your vulnerabilities (e.g., fatigue, intoxication)

-Be wary of strangers who offer you something that seems too good to be true (e.g., free drinks, accommodations, or tours).
-Research your destination and stay informed about local scams and safety concerns. Stay in well-lit, tourist-friendly areas, especially at night.

-Keep your hotel room door locked and secure and use the hotel's safe if available. Keep your valuables secure and be mindful of your belongings, especially in crowded areas.

-Avoid traveling alone at night or in isolated areas. Don't leave drinks unattended or accept them from strangers.

-Keep your phone charged and accessible in case of emergencies.

-Stay in touch with family and friends back home and let them know your itinerary.

-Trust your instincts – if a situation feels uncomfortable or suspicious, remove yourself from it immediately.

**Additional tips:**

- Research key hand/ body signals, for saying 'Help!'
- Carry a portable charger and a whistle or other noise-making device.
- Consider using a money belt or secure wallet.
- Don't display signs of wealth (e.g., expensive jewelry, watches, or large amounts of cash).

**List the phone numbers for local emergency service below. (Use pencil)**

## Police Department, Fire Department, Non-Emergency Line & Roadside Assistance

"Your intuition is the whisper of your soul, guiding you through life's uncertainties."
 -Unknown

## { 13 }

# SHARE YOUR LOCATION

Sharing your location with a trusted person is not just a technological convenience—it is an essential safety precaution, especially when traveling solo. By keeping a close connection with someone who knows your whereabouts at all times, you create a virtual safety net that can alert authorities or loved ones if anything goes awry. The knowledge that someone is aware of your exact location can be a game-changer in emergencies, particularly when you are in unfamiliar or high-risk environments where immediate assistance may be scarce.

Traveling in new places can sometimes evoke a sense of vulnerability, and having a reliable contact monitoring your location can provide both practical support and emotional comfort. When you share your location, you invite your trusted contact to offer advice and guidance based on their knowledge of the area or even suggest alternative routes if you recount any difficulties you encounter. This real-time connectivity strengthens your ability to navigate challenging situations, making you less isolated and more empowered by the security of knowing help is just a message away.

Beyond the immediate safety benefits, sharing your location plays a significant role in bridging the distance between you and your loved ones. It transforms a solo journey into one that feels shared, reassuring those back home that you are safe and present. The peace of mind that flow from knowing someone is keeping track of your movements cannot be overstated. It allows you to fully immerse yourself in your travel experiences without the nagging worry about your safety on remote roads or in unknown neighborhoods. Your loved ones, in turn, can maintain their connection to your journey, feeling more secure even when you are exploring far from familiar surroundings.

In the digital age, practical tools have made location sharing incredibly simple. Services like Life 360® offer the ability to track individuals or groups for free, indefinitely, making them an ideal choice for continuous monitoring during extended trips. Additionally, iPhone® users can share their location through built-in features, choosing to do so for a limited period or indefinitely based on personal preference and the demands of the trip. These tools not only provide accurate, real-time updates but also help establish a clear line of communication that can be critical in moments when directions or emergency measures are needed.

By choosing to share your location with someone who is proactive and available, you foster an added layer of security that turns your solo adventure into a journey that is both connected and safe. This simple act of communication ensures that, should you ever find yourself in a predicament, someone is immediately aware of your situation and can take swift action to help. Knowing that someone else is looking out for you allows you to savor the excitement of travel while remaining prepared for any unexpected twists along the way.

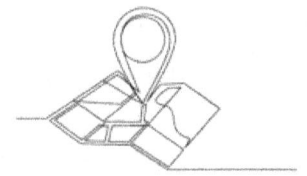

## { 14 }

# PROTECT YOUR BELONGINGS

To ensure a worry-free and enjoyable vacation, it's essential to take necessary precautions to protect your belongings. Always be mindful of your surroundings, keep valuables secure and out of sight, use hotel safes or lockers when available, and consider investing in travel insurance that covers loss or theft.

### HANDBAGS

Most of us love a good handbag, and we love matching them with cute outfits, shoes and accessories. If you want to safeguard your valuables, consider ditching the shoulder bag for a crossbody bag. Opt for a spacious crossbody bag that can fit your must-haves, such as your phone, keys, wallet, pepper spray and headphones. This practical choice allows you to wear your bag in front of you, always keeping it within your line of sight. Plus, its secure design makes it more difficult for potential thieves to grab and go, giving you peace of mind while out and about.

### BACKPACKS

Those adorable miniature backpacks may be stylish, but they often compromise on security, leaving your valuable belongings vulnerable. Many are made with rigid materials that make it difficult to detect if someone has secretly unzipped them. And because they're worn behind you, you might not even realize your items are missing until you remove the bag.

Be aware that pickpockets are becoming increasingly sophisticated. For added peace of mind, consider using a regular backpack with a secure zipper lock to protect your essentials.

## RFID BLOCKERS

Did you know that a simple bump or brush from a stranger can be enough for a skilled thief to drain your bank account? This can happen when your credit or debit cards with 'Tap' technology, also known as contactless payment cards, are stored in your wallet or purse.

To protect yourself from this type of theft, consider using RFID (Radio Frequency Identification) blocker sleeves on all your cards with Tap technology. These sleeves create a secure barrier between your cards and the thieves' scanning devices, preventing them from accessing your sensitive financial information.

By using RFID blocker sleeves, you can safeguard your money and enjoy the convenience of contactless payments with peace of mind. You can find them on Amazon for under $15.

## HOTEL ROOM SAFES

Utilizing a hotel safe is a simple yet effective way to protect your valuables while traveling. By storing your important documents, cash, credit cards, and other precious items in the safe, you can enjoy peace of mind knowing that they are secure and protected from theft or loss.

Hotel safes are typically designed with advanced security features, such as digital locks and tamper-evident mechanisms, making it difficult for unauthorized individuals to access your belongings. Additionally, using a hotel safe can also help to reduce your liability in case of theft, as you can demonstrate that you took reasonable steps to protect your property.

By taking advantage of this convenient and secure storage option, you can focus on enjoying your trip without worrying about the safety of your valuables.

## PREVENT SMASH & GRAB

To avoid becoming a victim of smash and grab, it's essential to be mindful of your surroundings and take necessary precautions. When parking your vehicle, choose a well-lit and populated area, avoiding isolated or dark spots. Avoid leaving valuables such as purses, laptops, or phones in plain sight, as this can attract unwanted attention.

Instead, keep them out of sight or take them with you. Additionally, consider using a car safe or locking your valuables in the trunk to add an extra layer of security. When stopping at intersections or traffic lights, be cautious of your surroundings and keep your doors and windows locked. Avoid engaging with suspicious individuals or distractions, such as someone approaching your vehicle or creating a commotion.

Keep your valuables close and be prepared to drive away quickly if necessary. By being aware of your
surroundings and taking proactive measures, you can minimize the risk of becoming a victim of smash and grab.

**Other Tips & Tricks**

-Keep your hotel room door locked and secure, even when inside.

-Use a doorstop or wedge to prevent unauthorized entry Out and About.

-Be mindful of your surroundings and keep valuables close.

-Avoid carrying large amounts of cash; use credit cards or traveler's checks instead.

-Keep your valuables organized and easily accessible.

-Consider using a tracking device (e.g., Tile, Find My Phone) for valuable items.

-Stay informed about local scams and safety concerns.

-Tampon Trick: Conceal emergency cash by rolling it tightly and placing it in an unused tampon applicator. Slide it back into the wrapper for discreet storage.

# { 15 }

# PET ACCOMODATIONS

Are you a pet owner who hates leaving your furry friend behind when you travel? You're not alone! Many pet owners consider their pets part of the family and want to bring them along on adventures. With some planning and preparation, you can ensure a safe and enjoyable trip for both you and your pet.

## CHOOSING PET FRIENDLY DESTINATIONS

Not all destinations are created equal when it comes to pet-friendliness. Research your destination to ensure it welcomes pets. Look for pet-friendly hotels, beaches, parks, and restaurants.

## PREPARING YOUR PET FOR TRAVEL

1. Get a health certificate for your pet within 10 days of travel.
2. Ensure your pet's vaccinations are up to date.
3. Microchip your pet for easy identification.
4. Acclimate your pet to their carrier or crate.
5. Pack your pet's favorite toys, food, and medication.

## TRANSPORTING YOUR PET

-By Car: Start by getting your pet accustomed to their carrier or harness, and ensure it's securely fastened in the vehicle. Pack your pet's favorite toys, treats, and blankets to provide a sense of familiarity, and bring along a portable food and water bowl, as well as a supply of their regular food and medication. Plan regular breaks every few hours to let your pet stretch, exercise, and use the bathroom, and consider booking pet-friendly hotels or accommodations along the way. Don't forget to keep your pet's identification and vaccination records easily accessible and consider investing in a pet first-aid kit and a portable crate for added peace of mind.

- By Air: When boarding an airplane with a pet, it's crucial to follow the airline's specific rules and regulations. Generally, small pets in approved carriers can travel in the cabin with their owner, while larger pets may need to travel as checked baggage or cargo. Owners must obtain a health certificate for their pet within 10 days of travel and ensure their pet's vaccinations are up to date. The pet carrier must fit under the seat in front of the owner and meet the airline's size requirements. Owners must also notify the airline in advance and pay any applicable pet fees. Additionally, emotional support animals and service animals have different requirements, so it's essential to check with the airline for their policies.

-By Train/Bus: Research pet policies for public transportation. Generally, small pets in carriers are allowed
on trains and buses, but there may be restrictions on size, type, and number of pets per passenger. Some transportation providers, like Amtrak, allow pets in designated pet-friendly cars, while others, like Greyhound, only permit service animals.

Pets may need to be in an approved carrier that fits under the seat or in a designated pet area. Additional fees may apply, and owners must keep their pets under control and clean up after them. It's essential to research and understand the pet policy before booking your ticket.

## PET TRAVEL ESSENTIALS:

1. Food and water bowls
2. Food and treats
3. Medication and supplements
4. Favorite toys and blankets
5. Pet first-aid kit
6. Poo bags and cleaning supplies

## TIPS FOR A STRESS-FREE TRIP

1. Plan regular breaks for exercise and potty stops.
2. Keep your pet calm with familiar items and treats.
3. Research pet-friendly activities and attractions.
4. Consider hiring a pet sitter or asking a friend to check in on your pet if you're away from your accommodation.

## LEAVING YOUR PET AT HOME

If you can't take your pet with you on a trip, arranging for their care at home can provide peace of mind. Consider hiring a trusted pet sitter or asking a reliable friend or

family member to check in on your pet regularly. This way, your pet can maintain their routine and stay in the comfort of their own environment.

When accommodating your pet at home, make sure to leave clear instructions for their caregiver, including feeding schedules, medication administration, and contact information for your veterinarian.

Stock up on food, treats, and supplies to ensure your pet's needs are met, and consider investing in a pet camera to monitor their activity remotely.

For added convenience, consider hiring a pet sitter who can also take care of your home while you're away, such as collecting mail and watering plants, whilst simultaneously keeping your pet away from toxic plants.

Alternatively, some pet sitters offer overnight stays, providing your pet with companionship and attention throughout the night.

### FOR CATS

You could invest in an automatic feeder that can hold enough food for your time away from home.

An extra litter box can alleviate some stress for both you and your cat(s).

# IN CLOSING

As this book comes to a close, I invite you to reflect on the empowering journey you're about to embark on. Traveling as a woman means embracing every facet of adventure—whether it's exploring vibrant urban centers, safe and scenic countryside escapes, or hidden local gems that invite you to dive deep into rich cultures and experiences. You've discovered that a well-prepared itinerary, coupled with smart financial strategies, can transform your travel dreams into reality. By wisely saving for your trip and learning to prioritize experiences over fleeting material pleasures, you create a foundation that enables you to travel more often and live your best life on the road.

Safety is the cornerstone of every journey. From the detailed precautions in choosing secure accommodations and sharing your location with a trusted person, to the everyday decisions that bolster your personal well-being, you've learned that being proactive about safety isn't about living in fear—it's about empowering yourself. Every tip and personal anecdote in these pages is a reminder that your safety matters, and that embracing thoughtful caution allows you to explore more boldly and with greater freedom. Whether traveling solo, as part of a close-knit group of like-minded women, or while accompanied by children and even pets, you deserve to experience travel without compromise.

Your adventures have no boundaries, and the cities and attractions recommended throughout this book are but a glimpse of what awaits you. Imagine wandering through bustling city streets filled with history and art, discovering peaceful parks and serene beaches that evoke a sense of wonder, or setting out on a scenic road trip where every sunrise promises a new beginning. Each destination, whether renowned or off the beaten path, carries its own unique allure and offers an opportunity to forge connections and create unforgettable memories. It's in these moments of exploration that you not only discover new places but also unveil deeper layers of yourself.

Traveling with children or pets adds another beautiful dimension to your journey, inviting you to share the wonder of discovery with those you care about most. Whether it's the excitement in a child's eyes as they marvel at a historic landmark or the comfort of having a beloved pet by your side on a long day of sightseeing, these shared moments enrich your experience in ways that are both unexpected and deeply rewarding. At the same time, venturing out in groups of women or along with supportive friends provides a sense of unity and collective strength, making the challenges of travel less daunting and the joys even more vibrant.

In closing, remember that your journey as a traveler is a personal tapestry woven from safety, smart planning, and the courage to venture into the unknown. Whether you're setting out on a solo expedition or gathering with a tight circle of kindred spirits, the world is full of opportunities waiting for you to explore. Let this book serve as both a guide and a reminder that every step you take is a celebration of your strength, independence, and zest for life. Your adventure awaits—step into it with confidence, and let every destination be a chapter in your own remarkable story.

## { 16 }

# BONUS SECTION- PACKING ESSENTIALS

If you can pack everything you need into a carry-on bag, a weekender bag might be the perfect fit. The only downside is that weekender bags are usually shoulder bags which means you have to carry them around. They can be pretty heavy once you add shoes and toiletries.

If you decide to use it as carry-on you have to make sure that everything you packed is allowed onboard.

As mentioned before, Southwest Airlines® allows two free checked bags. So, take advantage of that if you can.

What you'll need:

1. Compression bags- These reusable plastic bags allow you to neatly fold your clothing, place them in the bag, seal it tightly then roll it to release all of the air

and flatten the bag. (No need to use a vacuum) They will save you so much space in your luggage!
2. Shoe bags- These bags hold up to 2 pairs of shoes each, keeping them clean and from touching your clothing.
3. Toiletry bags- These usually come in multi-packs so you can separate your toiletries. Use one bag for your travel toothbrush and facial care products, a second one for your makeup and a third for your body products like, body wash, deodorant, lotion, perfumes etc.
4. Luggage tags- The more unique the better. Luggage tags help you spot your bags quickly at baggage claim since a lot of luggage can look alike. Look for ones with a hideaway tag to write your personal information on in case Airline personnel need to contact you.

# { 17 }

# BONUS SECTION- WHERE TO EAT

If you're a foodie like me, and you also love watching shows where the host visits restaurants and tries their top menu items, try googling your destination to find out if they visited any of the restaurants in that town.

Once you see some things you want to try, list the restaurant names and menu items below: (use pencil)

------------------------------------------------
------------------------------------------------
------------------------------------------------
------------------------------------------------
------------------------------------------------
------------------------------------------------
------------------------------------------------
------------------------------------------------
------------------------------------------------
-----------------------------------------

## { 18 }

# BONUS SECTION- STRANGERS

**HARMLESS LIES TO TELL STRANGERS WHILE ON VACATION:**

"I'm here with my husband/fiancé/boyfriend."

"I'm meeting friends/family here."

"I'm only here for a day/night."

"I have an early tour/appointment."

"I'm not feeling well."

"I'm on a work trip" (to appear less available)

"I'm traveling with a group" (even if you are alone)

"I need to go charge my phone/camera" (to excuse yourself)

## 7 THINGS YOU CAN SAY TO SET CLEAR BOUNDARIES:

Please respect my personal space."

"I don't want to go out/exploring with you."

"I'm not looking for company/ friendship/ romance."

"Please don't touch/hug/meet me."

"I'm not comfortable with this conversation."

"I'd prefer not to discuss my personal life."

"I'm going to go now, please don't follow me."

**Remember to:**

- Be firm but polite
- Maintain eye contact
- Use a strong, assertive tone
- Avoid apologetic or hesitant language

- Prioritize your safety and comfort


**For fun, try:**
-Inventing an eccentric profession
-Claiming an unusual hometown
-Makeing up a celebrity connection
-Creating a bizarre personal tradition
-Pretending to be a world record holder
-Giving an absurd food recommendation
-Inventing a completely imaginary festival you plan to attend soon.

## { 19 }

# BONUS SECTION- PERSONAL SAFETY

THINGS TO CARRY AT ALL TIMES TO KEEP YOU SAFE.

(Check with airlines about restrictions for checked bags.

- Pepper spray or personal alarm
- Whistle or other loud noise making device.
- Portable charger for phone or other devices
- Money belt or secure wallet
- Copies of important documents (i.e. passport, ID, travel insurance)
- Emergency contact information and phone numbers
- Small first aid kit
- Travel-sized self-defense tools.
- Comfortable and secure clothing and shoes
- Guidebook or map with important phone numbers and addresses

- Hotel room key card backup
- Snacks and water to stay energized.
- Small flashlight or extra batteries
- Personal safety app (e.g. bSafe® Life360®)

Travel insurance information and emergency contact details.

## { 20 }

# BONUS SECTION- ITINERARY

## SAMPLE DAILY ITINERARY

For those who have a list of places to visit that don't require reservations.

**Location:** Las Vegas
**Day 1:**
**Places to visit:**
"Welcome to Fabulous Las Vegas" Sign
Mandalay Bay Casino
Republica Statue of Liberty:
Bellagio Conservatory and Botanical Gardens
Bellagio Fountains
The High Roller
Cirque Du Soleil
Caesar's Palace

**Day 2:**
**Places to visit:**
Red Rock Canyon
The Stratosphere Casino
Escape Blair Witch
Eiffel Tower Experience
**Day 3:**
**Places to visit:**
Seven Magic Mountains
Neon Museum
Downtown Las Vegas: Visit Fremont Street

## SAMPLE HOURLY ITINERARY

**For those who purchased tickets in advance and made reservations.**

The below Itinerary is half of the actual one I created for my Trip to New Orleans.

**Location:** New Orleans
**Saturday 11/11**
4pm- Check in to hotel
5:30pm- Visit Bourbon St/ dinner
7pm- Visit Carousel Bar
8pm- Make way back to Streetcar
9:30pm Bedtime

**Sunday 11/12**
8am-Wake up
8:15am Shower
9am- Small snack
10am- Streetcar
11am- Sunday Jazz Cruise Brunch
3pm- Southern Food & Beverage Museum
5pm- Botanical Garden/ dinner
7:30pm Preservation Hall Jazz show
9pm- Head back to Streetcar
10pm- Bedtime

# { 21 }

# BONUS SECTION- PLACES TO GO

Embracing my inner tourist, I delight in exploring new cities, soaking up their culture, and uncovering their historical treasures. Here's a state-by-state guide to popular tourist destinations that offer a mix of culture, history, and entertainment.

- **Birmingham, AL**

Mcwane Science Center, Birmingham Zoo, Pepper Place Saturday Market

- **Juneau, AK**

Alaska State Museum, Whale Watching, Bear Viewing

- **Phoenix, AZ**

Musical Instrument Museum, Area Science Center, Heritage Square.

- **Eureka Springs, AR**

Intrigue Theater, Quigley's Castle, Onyx Cave

- **San Diego, CA**

Balboa Park, Oldtown San Diego, Sunset Cliffs

- **Boulder, CO**

Eldorado Canyon State Park, Boulder Creek Path, Pearl Street Mall

- **Hartford, CT**

The Mark Twain House & Museum, Butler-McCook House & Garden, Bushnell Park Carousel

- **Wilmington, DE**

The Grand Opera House, Bellevue State Park, Delaware Art Museum.

- **Orlando, FL**

Disney World, The Orlando Eye, Orlando Museum of Art.

- **Atlanta, GA**

Atlanta Botanical Gardens, World of Coca-Cola, Fox Theatre

- **Honolulu, HI**

Manoa Falls, Kualoa Ranch, Diamond head State Monument.

- **Boise, ID**

Camels Back Park, Idaho Botanical Garden, Aquarium of Boise.

- **Chicago, IL**

Wrigley Field, Navy Pier, Riverwalk

- **Indianapolis, IN**

White River State Park, Victory Field, Monument Circle

- **Iowa City, IA**

Old Capitol Museum, Devonian Fossil Gorge, Amana Colonies

- **Wichita, KS**

Botanica, Museum of World Treasures, Old Town Square.

- **Lexington, KY**

Kentucky Horse Park, Mary Todd Lincoln House, McConnell Springs Park

- **New Orleans, LA**

Jackson Square, French Quarter, New Orleans Museum of Art

- **Portland, ME**

Victoria Mansion, Portland head Light, Commercial Street

- **Baltimore, MD**

Patterson Park, American Visionary Art Museum, B&O Railroad Museum

- **Cambridge, MA**

Harvard Square, MIT Museum, Fenway Park

- **Ann Arbor, MI**

Matthaei Botanical Gardens, Hudson Hills Metropark, Law Quadrangle

- **Jackson, MS**

Governor's Mansion, Old Capitol Museum, Mississippi Agriculture & Forestry Museum

- **St. Paul, MN**

James J Hill House, St Paul's Farmers' Market, Rice Park

- **Kansas City, MO**

American Jazz Museum, Negro League Baseball Museum, Country Club Plaza

- **Bozeman, MT**

Bozeman Hot Springs, Peets Hill/ Burke Park, Bozeman Spirits Distillery, Yellowstone National Park is less than 2 hours away.

- **Omaha, NE**

Joslyn Castle & Gardens, The Old Market, Kiewit Luminarium

- **Las Vegas/ Reno, NV**

Fremont Street Experience, The Mob Museum, Las Vegas Strip, The Discovery, Truckee River Walk, Idlewild Park

- **N. Conway, NH**

Conway Scenic Railroad, Diana's Bath, Story Land

- **Cape May, NJ**

Cape May Lighthouse, Harriet Tubman Museum, Jersey Shore Alpacas

- **Santa Fe, NM**

Santa Fe Plaza, Museum of International Folk Art, Meow Wolf Santa FE

- **New York City, NY**

Empire State Building, Brooklyn Bridge, Central park

- **Charlotte, NC**

SouthPark, Charlotte Motor Speedway, Billy Graham Library

- **Fargo, ND**

Fargo Air Museum, West Acres Mall, Drekker Brewing Company

- **Cincinnati, OH**

Cincinnati Music Hall, Washington Park, Cincinnati Observatory

- **Oklahoma City, OK**

Bricktown Water Taxi, American Banjo Museum, Factory Obscura Mix-Tape

- **Portland, OR**

Portland Japanese Garden, The Grotto, International Rose Test Garden

- **Philadelphia, PA**

Liberty Bell, Rocky Statue, Franklin Square

- **Newport, RI**

Bowen's Wharf, Cliff Walk- South End, Thames Street

- **Charleston, SC**

Charleston City Park, White Point Garden, Fort Sumter National Monument

- **Sioux Falls, SD**

Sculpture Walk, Butterfly House & Aquarium, USS South Dakota Battleship Memorial

- **Nashville, TN**

Country Music Hall of Fame and Museum, Johnny Cash Museum, Grand Ole Opry

- **Austin, TX**

Lady Bird lake, Zilker Botanical Garden, Texas Capitol

- **Zion National Park, UT**

Canyon Overlook Trail, The Narrows, Angels Landing

- **WoodStock, VT**

Sugarbush Farm, Middle Covered Bridge, Marsh - Billings - Rockefeller National Historical Park

- **Virginia Beach, VA**

Neptune's Park, First Landing State Park, Hunt Club Farm

- **Seattle, WA**

Museum of Pop Culture, Space Needle, Skyview Observatory

- **Fayetteville, WV**

New River Gorge National Park, Long Point Trail, Historic Fayette Theater

- **Sheboygan, WI**

Bookworm Gardens, Breaker bay Waterpark, Art Preserve of the John Michael Kohler Arts Center

- **Jackson, WY**

Jackson Town Square, Jackson Hole Rodeo, Grand Teton National Park

## Which States have you visited so far?

_____
_____
_____
_____
_____
_____

# ABOUT THE AUTHOR

Nita is a new Jersey native, currently residing in California. She wears many hats, including Mother, Entrepreneur, Designer, Bookkeeper, Tax Professional, Real Estate Agent and most recently, Published Author. She is a foodie and a lover of culture who looks for any reason to get out of town for a few days.

# NOTES

www.ingramcontent.com/pod-product-compliance
Lightning Source LLC
LaVergne TN
LVHW051953060526
838201LV00059B/3623